Tennessee Ghosts

they are among us

Lynne L. Hall

SWEETWATER
PRESS

Tennessee Ghosts

SWEETWATER
    PRESS

Tennessee Ghosts
Copyright © 2006 by Sweetwater Press
Produced by Cliff Road Books

ISBN-13: 978-1-58173-566-6
ISBN-10: 1-58173-566-9

Book design by Pat Covert

Printed in the United States of America

Table of Contents

They Are Among Us

They Are Among Us

I won't lie to you. I'm a skeptic. I mean, like everyone else, I grew up shivering delightedly to ghost stories. But for the most part, I believed my mama when she told me, "There're no such things as ghosts."

Later on, I spent a lot of time examining the world around me and trying to fit it all into one mold or the other. Religion? Or science? The great debate. One entirely spiritual, based on faith. The other, entirely logical, based on scientific evidence.

For many years, I fell solidly on the science side. It was that scientific evidence thing that got me. So I spent a lot of time and effort ignoring the things that didn't fit my mold, chalking them up to coincidence or serendipity.

But years bring wisdom, and, if you're lucky, they open your heart and mind. I was lucky. I had an experience with the spiritual realm, a realm we can't see or touch but know in our hearts exists.

It happened days after the death of Oleta, a woman who was dear to me, a woman who'd parented me as much, if not more, than my own parents. In the performance of my duties as a professional firefighter, I was about to go into a burning house. At the moment I crawled over the threshold, I heard Oleta's voice in my head: "Be careful, Lynne." In that moment I knew she was there, watching over me.

That experience brought a realization, that, yes, there's scientific evidence for some things. But there're many other things that simply can't be explained by science, things that can only be known in your own heart. I found there was a place for both realms; that the spiritual could exist side by side with the logical.

Still, when it came to actual ghosts, ones that you have no connection to, that appeared and disappeared and made strange noises, I remained skeptical. So I approached this project with a sense of fun, searching out stories that would be fun to tell and entertaining to read.

I found them, I think, but I also found something else. I found a collection of stories with common threads. In each story, there was a strong connection between the spirits and the places they were haunting. And, there was something in their lives that, in death, seems to keep them bound to this world. Perhaps the death was a violent or sudden one. Or perhaps there was a loss of a great love. Whatever the reason, they're here. And they've made themselves known. They've been seen. They've been heard. And they can't be explained away by science.

The more I researched this book, the more I became convinced of the "reality" of ghosts like the Indian princess Nocatula and her beloved Conestoga; the soldiers who died on the property of the Carter Family of Franklin in one of the bloodiest battles of the Civil War; or the young firl, Mary, who haunts the orpheum Theater in Memphis.

It's enough to make a skeptic wonder if, indeed, they are among us.

Lynne L. Hall

The Legend of Nocatula

The Legend of Nocatula

No, Mocking Crow. I've told you, I do not love you, and I cannot marry you," Cherokee Princess Nocatula Cooweena sighed. She truly wished the man would leave her alone. She could never marry him. His arrogance alone would've been enough to keep her from ever feeling anything but contempt for him, but on top of that, he was a mean-spirited man.

A member of the Deer Clan, he was responsible for the care of the tribe's animals, but she had seen him lose his temper and kick or hit them numerous times. She often scolded him for it. With humans, he was quick to anger and would readily draw his knife at any provocation. It was just a matter of time before he actually killed someone, she knew.

"But I have brought you this beautiful gift. You do not like it?"

"It is beautiful, as you say. But I cannot accept it." She handed the ring back to him. Carved from shell and intricately decorated, it would make a lovely gift, had it come from someone she loved. Mocking Crow took the ring and, his face dark with anger, left her without another word.

Chief Attakulla-Kulla was approaching. He gave Mocking Crow a long look as he passed him.

"You've turned down Mocking Crow's proposal again?" He smiled at his daughter.

"Yes, Father. I wish he would leave me alone. I could never marry him."

Her father nodded. "I would not choose Mocking Crow for you. He feeds the wrong wolf."

Nocatula smiled, remembering the ancient story of the two wolves living inside each of us—one of evil, full of anger, envy, arrogance, and ego; and the other of good, full of benevolence, joy, and peace. The two wolves are at war with each other. Which one wins? The one you feed. Mocking Crow was definitely feeding the wrong one, she thought.

"There are many worthy young braves who would gladly ask for your hand, if you'd just give them a sign," he continued.

"I know, Father. But none of them speaks to my heart."

Attakulla smiled and nodded. His beautiful daughter was strong on having a man who spoke to

13

her heart. But as chief of the Wolf Clan, he was anxious for her to start raising little warriors. "Let's hope, my daughter, that your heart starts listening before the Great Spirit calls me."

Nocatula laughed. "You are but a young brave, Father. There's plenty of time yet."

Little did either realize that in a few days' time, the father would find himself bewildered, and his daughter's heart would be singing. It all happened when Attakulla accompanied a hunting party into the deep woods surrounding their village.

At the beginning of the day, he sighted a pack of wolves shadowing their party, and it put his senses on alert. As chief of the Wolf Clan, the warriors of the Cherokee, the wolves were his brothers. Throughout the day, the pack stayed near, showing themselves briefly, then disappearing. Attakulla knew it to be an omen.

The hunt went well, with the young braves taking three deer, which were loaded onto a litter for the trip back to the village. As they rode noisily through the woods, the braves bragging and laughing about their kills, Attakulla was silent. He knew that somewhere on the trip back was something—he didn't know what— that his brothers, the wolves, wanted him to find.

14

They had almost made it back to the village when one of the party let out a shout.

They halted, and Attakulla rode up from the back. What he found up front had silenced the members of the hunting party, but it didn't surprise him.

Lying face down in the underbrush was a white man. His white shirt was bloodstained, and his yellow hair was matted red. But that wasn't what had stunned the braves into silence. There was a lone she-wolf sitting next to the man. Her blue eyes found Attakulla and held him in her gaze for a long moment. She then turned and disappeared into the woods.

Amid protests from the hunting party, the chief slid from his pony and knelt beside the white man. The man was unconscious, but he still lived. Attakulla ordered that he be loaded onto the litter and brought back to the village. The senior members of the hunting party wanted to protest, but the she-wolf had unnerved them. They agreed with Chief Attakulla. It had to be an omen.

A shout went up as they rode into the village, and by the time they reached the small shelter reserved for guests, half the town was following them.

"Take him inside," Attakulla ordered. "You, child, go get the medicine man." The little boy went running off.

Nocatula hurried up. "What is it, Father? Are you all right?"

"Yes, daughter. I am fine. Our wolf brothers have led us to a wounded white man. We have brought him back for care, as they wished."

Curious, Nocatula entered the shelter. The white man lay silently on a pallet of hides. Dirt and blood streaked his face. His clothes were torn. She knelt beside him and began removing his shirt, noting the mat of gold hair covering his chest. How strange, she thought. The chests of the Cherokee were smooth and hairless.

A bowl full of warm water was brought, and she began bathing the blood and dirt away from his face and chest. As she worked, she couldn't help but take in his strangeness—the hair of gold, and his skin, which, though white, seemed to have a golden tint as well. She'd seen white men, of course, but not up close like this.

As she ran the warm cloth over his face, his eyes opened briefly, and she sat back in surprise. They were blue! As blue as the morning sky! "Who are you?" he whispered before falling back into unconsciousness.

At the sound of his voice, a thrill passed through her, setting her body a-tingle and causing a flutter in her chest. A gasp escaped her. "He has spoken to my heart," she thought.

The medicine man came. He administered his potions, and chanted and danced his medicine dance. Nocatula sat in the back of the shelter, watching the man as the healing rituals were being performed. He opened his eyes several times, registering alarm as the medicine man passed smoking herbs over his body, but then passing out again each time.

After the medicine man left, Nocatula finished bathing the man and covered him with blankets. She crept from the shelter to find her father in council with the tribe elders. The wolf omen confused them, but they accepted that there was a reason to bring the white stranger into the village. It was decided that he would stay and be nursed back to health, if possible. The wolf brother would reveal his purpose in time.

For several days, there was no change as the stranger drifted in and out of consciousness. Each time he woke, he saw the beautiful face of an angel. Sometimes he would reach up and touch that face. It seemed so real. He could actually feel the soft skin,

17

and run his fingers through the silky black hair. He could feel gentle hands bathing his face and chest with warm, fragrant water.

Finally, one morning he woke, with a head that felt like a smashed melon, but with his wits about him. He had no idea where he was or how he got there. Examining the colorful blanket covering him, he noted that he was lying on a pallet of animal hides. Obviously, Indians had captured him, but how and why? And what did they plan to do with him?

He sat up, still trying to remember what happened to him. The last thing he remembered was riding through the forest, and the next thing he knew, he woke up here.

"You're awake!" He turned just as she stepped into the shelter. It was his beautiful Indian maiden angel. He remembered her from his dreams. She was wearing a soft, fringed deerskin dress and carrying a bowl.

"Lie back down. You're too weak to be up."

"Where am I?"

"You are with the Cherokee nation," she replied.

"I'm a captive?"

"No, of course not. We found you in the forest and brought you here."

"Then, you've been taking care of me?"

"Yes. You've been walking with the spirits for many days."

She came inside and placed the bowl on a small table beside him. It was some type of stew, and its aroma suddenly made him realize that he was starving. He looked around for eating utensils, but there were none.

Seeing his confusion, Nocatula picked up the bowl, and, taking a piece of bread, demonstrated using the bread to pick up the stew, then handed him the bowl. As she watched him eat, she listened to the singing in her heart, a singing that had begun in the days she'd nursed him, when he'd gently touched her face and fingered her hair.

"What do your people call you?" she asked.

He stopped eating and searched his mind. Nothing came to him.

"I don't seem to remember. What about my things? Was there anything in them?"

She pointed to his clothes in the corner. "No. Only what you wore. Nothing else." A quick examination revealed that he was a British soldier.

Though the throbbing in his head was like a hammer against his eyeballs, he tried to think. There was nothing. He remembered nothing about who he was or about his past.

"Do not worry. In time the spirits may give back your memory. Until then, we'll call you Conestoga. It means 'oak.' It's also the name of the big wagons that carry your people to the western lands." She took the empty bowl from his hands. "Rest now. Tomorrow you can try to walk."

He laid back into the piled up skins and watched her as she straightened up the small shelter. She was a beautiful woman, exotic with her dark skin and shining black hair that spilled over her shoulders and down her back. Remembering her gentleness as she nursed him, a profound gratitude filled him. Or perhaps it was more than gratitude, for despite the pounding of his head and his fear at having lost his memory, his heart felt lighter. Maybe, he thought, maybe there is a reason I was brought here. As the thought entered his mind, he saw fearsome fangs and glowing red eyes. Why, he wondered, would his only memory be of a wolf?

Weeks passed and Conestoga's mind and body healed. His memory returned, and he knew that he was heir to a vast estate in England, and that as a

British soldier, he'd been well-known for his bravery on the battlefield. He remembered that robbers had ambushed him and left him for dead in the forest. And he remembered flashes of a huge wolf standing over him as he lay dying.

The longer he stayed, living among what, until now, he had thought of as "savages," the less he wanted to return to his old life. Far from being savage, the Cherokee, he found, had established their own government, had their own constitution, and had a written language. Their children went to school, just as "civilized" English children, and there was a court system. He did, in fact, find them more civilized than the courtiers he'd known.

All that, of course, was not the real reason he didn't want to leave. The real reason was that he'd fallen completely, deeply, madly in love with Princess Nocatula. She was beautiful and charming, and she had his heart clutched firmly in her hands. Best of all, she felt the same about him.

He knew that their obvious love for each other troubled many of her people. But other than making a comment or two, they seemed to stay away from the subject. Nocatula told him it was because of the wolf that stood over him that day in the forest. They saw it as an omen.

Conestoga saw the truth in that belief. He knew some wild quirk of fate had led him there. He was supposed to be here, to love this woman and to live his life in peace here with her. He didn't care about anything else—the English estate, his commission as a British officer, none of that mattered. He just wanted to be here with her and her people. No doubt, the people of his old life thought him dead. That was just fine with him.

Several months passed. Then, on one starry night, Conestoga approached Attakulla as he sat smoking his pipe in front of the campfire. Hands slick with nervous sweat, he asked for Nocatula's hand in marriage. He and the old Indian had become close friends in the past weeks, but marriage to a man's daughter was quite a different matter. He wasn't sure what he would do if his request was denied. But the chief nodded and puffed on his pipe.

"My daughter has long searched for someone who speaks to her heart, but her heart could hear nothing from our braves. Our wolf brothers brought you here for her. It's not for me to deny her the brave who speaks to her heart."

Nocatula Cooweena and Conestoga were married in a beautiful weeklong celebration of singing and dancing. According to tradition, as they took their vows, each was covered with a blue blanket. When the vows were completed, the priestess removed the blue blankets and covered the couple with the traditional white blanket, signifying their union.

The couple settled into their new home and began their life together. So happy were they that they ignored the growing animosity of Mocking Crow. His jealousy had quickly turned to a hatred that ate away at his insides. Every day, he saw his coveted Nocatula walking hand in hand with the white stranger and gazing at him with love in her eyes. Every day, his hatred grew until his heart was black.

Mocking Crow knew in his black heart that if the white man had not shown up, the lovely Nocatula would have accepted his proposal. No one else was worthy. She would have seen that eventually. But all was not lost. He had a plan to get rid of the white stranger. Nocatula would yet be his. And since it had all begun with a hunting party, it was only fitting that it all end with one.

Conestoga was exhilarated over the success of the

autumn hunt. Ten deer had been killed. There would be plenty of meat to cure and store for the winter. And he was pleased that his practice with the bow had paid off. Two of the deer were his kills. He was happy to be a contributing member of his new community. A quiet peace filled him as he walked through the forest, leading his pony.

A noise in the bushes made him stop. Suddenly, in front of him, he saw a wolf, its eyes glowing red. It growled, then disappeared back in the bushes. Had he been Cherokee, he would have seen the appearance of the wolf as an omen. He may have then altered his route, may have been more cautious. But he was a white man, and despite the time spent with the Cherokee, he saw only a wolf.

He continued on ahead of the party. Suddenly, a man stepped from the cover of the trees. It was Mocking Crow. Before Conestoga had a chance to react, Mocking Crow was upon him, knife drawn. Conestoga felt an incredible pain as the knife plunged into his chest. His knees buckled, and he fell to the ground, the knife still in his chest.

The hunting party found him there minutes later. "Nocatula..." he whispered.

A runner was sent back to the village, just yards away. Soon Nocatula was at his side, tears running down her face. He raised a hand and cradled her face.

"My Indian Princess. I love you…" His last words cut deep to her heart. She placed a tearful kiss on his still lips.

"My white warrior. I cannot live with a silent heart." Before anyone could stop her, she pulled the knife from his chest and plunged it into her heart. She fell across him, and for all the world, they looked like a couple sleeping peacefully on a pallet of pine straw.

That's how Attakulla found them. Grief-stricken, he ordered the couple buried on the spot where they had died. Before their grave was covered, he placed an acorn in Conestoga's hand. In his beloved Nocatula's hand, he placed a hackberry seed.

Within a year, the seeds had sprouted and a mighty oak tree grew next to a rounded hackberry tree. In 1857, a college later known as Tennessee Wesleyan was founded on the land that encompassed the two trees. Special care was taken in the construction to not disturb the trees. They stood for more than 165 years, at which time, the hackberry tree died and had to be cut down. Within the year, the oak tree, too, expired and was cut down. A sign now stands on the spot that tells the tale of Nocatula's and Conestoga's never-ending love.

Many believe their love lives on. Throughout the years, there have been countless reports of supernatural happenings on the site where the two trees once stood. Some report merely the sound of voices whispering. Others, however, report seeing two ghostly figures walking hand in hand in the darkness—the spirits, they say, of two lovers whose love has never died.

Meriwether Lewis Explores the Other Side

Meriwether Lewis Explores the Other Side

Was it murder most foul? Or was it suicide? For almost two hundred years, these questions have surrounded the death of explorer Meriwether Lewis of Lewis and Clark fame. The subject is a great debate among historians, and a multitude of theories abound.

Meriwether Lewis was a Virginian who served as secretary to fellow Virginian Thomas Jefferson. The two shared a Southern heritage and a fascination with the unexplored.

Jefferson acquired the Louisiana Purchase in 1803 and soon after, sent Lewis, who teamed with former army buddy William Clark, on an epic exploration journey to the Pacific Ocean. To prepare for the trip, Lewis studied navigation, plants, and animals at the University of Pennsylvania. In Jefferson's own words, "It was impossible to find a character who to a compleat science in botany, natural history, mineralogy, and astronomy, joined the firmness of constitution and character... and a familiarity with the Indian manners and character requisite for this undertaking." The Lewis and Clark Expedition was completed in 1806, and the two instantly became national heroes.

Jefferson granted Lewis the governorship of Louisiana to reward him, though Lewis may have thought it more punishment than reward. Despite his desire to ready the diaries he kept of the Lewis and Clark Expedition for publication, he immediately found himself mired in the duties and petty politics of the office. On top of his local problems, he also found the bureaucrats of Washington to be a royal pain. Not only did they refuse to approve vouchers for necessary expenditures, but they also impugned his integrity in making such requests.

Fed up, Lewis decided to kill two birds with one stone. He'd deliver the vouchers along with his official records in person and also deliver the Lewis and Clark diaries to the publishing company. He set off for Washington, leaving St. Louis by boat on September 4, 1809.

Not long after setting out, Lewis fell ill. Some speculate he suffered a recurrence of malaria. Others think he suffered a bout of depression, a condition he was known to have. And still others offer complete

29

speculation that he began experiencing dementia as a result of syphilis that he may or may not have contracted during the great expedition.

Whatever the cause, Lewis was in such a state that when the ship arrived in Fort Pickering on September 15, the captain decided to detain him there on a twenty-four-hour suicide watch.

Lewis recovered his wits in several days and, deciding to finish the trip over land, set out on September 29 toward Tennessee with government Indian agent James Neelly. They traveled on horseback for days and, as Neelly wrote to Jefferson in a letter, Lewis seemed "deranged" for much of the trip.

When they stopped to rest for a night after crossing the Tennessee River, two of their horses escaped. Neelly stayed behind to recapture the horses while Lewis went on ahead alone. He agreed to wait for Neelly at the first house he came to.

The first house Lewis came to was Grinder's Station, a small inn between Natchez and Nashville on the Natchez Trace, which Robert and Priscilla Grinder owned. When Lewis arrived, Robert was away and Priscilla was there with the couple's two children.

According to Mrs. Grinder in later accounts, the governor wasn't stable. He paced up and down, wildly talking to himself. He asked for liquor but hardly drank. He asked for food but barely ate. He would approach her purposefully, as if to tell her something, but would wheel away and continue his pacing. He was acting so strangely, she said, that she gave him the main house, taking her children to sleep in a smaller house next door.

Lewis refused to sleep in the bed, asking instead that his bearskins and buffalo robe be brought in. In the house just paces away, Mrs. Grinder said she was unable to sleep. She heard Lewis pacing back and forth, talking to himself "like a lawyer."

Sometime in the hours before dawn, a gunshot rang out and she heard a loud thud as if someone had fallen to the floor. She heard Lewis exclaim "Oh, Lord!" There was then another gunshot. A few minutes later, Lewis was at her door.

"Oh, Madam. Give me some water and heal my wounds!" he cried as he banged on the door.

Mrs. Grinder refused to open the door, an action that many question. Her story was that she was too frightened and worried for her children to open the door. She heard Lewis stumble away and, looking through the cracks in the logs, she saw him stagger back and fall against a stump. He rested there a few minutes, then crawled to a nearby tree and hauled himself up before stumbling back to the cabin.

Sometime later, Lewis returned to the door and again she refused to open it. Still looking through the cracks between the logs, she saw him stumble to the well, where she heard him scraping the bottom of the bucket with the gourd dipper in a vain effort to get water.

At daybreak, Mrs. Grinder finally emerged from the cabin. She found Lewis still conscious, lying on the bed. He was critically wounded with two gunshots. He had been shot in the side and the head. It was a gruesome sight. Part of his forehead had been blown away, exposing his brain.

If they would only take his rifle and finish him off, he pleaded, he would give them all the money he was carrying.

"I am no coward," he repeated over and over. "But I am so strong, so hard to die."

No one took Lewis up on his offer. Instead, they let him lie there until he died about two hours later.

When James Neelly arrived the next day, he buried Lewis there at Grinder's Station.

There's been much controversy about Lewis's death. The official inquest recorded the death as a suicide, and that verdict is accepted by most historians. However, even at the time of his death, there were questions about the circumstances. Many reject Mrs. Grinder's claim that she was frightened, and wonder why she refused assistance that night, a requirement of simple human decency.

They also point out that she changed her story, adding the arrival of three men, one of whom was Tom Runions, a known land pirate. One speculation is that Lewis was murdered by these men for his money.

Another story posits that Lewis was slain by a killer hired by General James Wilkinson. It seems that Lewis had information that Wilkinson was working with Aaron Burr, the famous traitor. The story is that Wilkinson had Lewis killed to prevent him from revealing that he, too, was a traitor.

Still other opinions were offered by the locals. One contingent believed that Robert Grinder was present that night, and that it was he who killed

Lewis for his money. The other contingent laughs at all other theories. They say it's obvious what happened: Robert Grinder came home unexpectedly that night and caught Lewis in bed with his wife and shot him. Everything else, they say, was made up by Mrs. Grinder.

It matters not whether Meriwether Lewis took his own life or whether unknown persons murdered him. Either way, it was a violent death. And a violent death often results in a restless spirit that has yet to find its way to the other side. This seems to be true of Lewis.

Lewis, who died on October 11, 1809, at age thirty-five, lay in an unmarked grave until 1848, when a marker was erected. Because of the remoteness of the area, however, it fell to disrepair. Finally, in 1925, a monument was erected over the grave, and the area around the site was declared the National Meriwether Lewis Monument.

Throughout this time, there have been reports of ghostly goings-on. Psychics who've explored the area have sighted and sensed the spirit of the great explorer. On dark nights, it's been said you can hear scraping sounds, as the sound of a gourd dipper being scraped against the bottom of a metal bucket. There have also

34

been the sounds of voices and whisperings. If you listen close enough as the wind riffles through the leaves, you might even hear the sound of Lewis's disembodied voice repeating his last words in life. Stand and listen and you may just hear the plaintive echo of "It is so hard to die."

The Story of the Bell Witch

The Story of the Bell Witch

No one knows for sure what ol' John Bell did to tick off his neighbor, Kate Batt. Speculation was that Kate was mad about either a land dispute or a disagreement over a sale of slaves. And she was so angry that even in death, she couldn't let it go. She vowed on her deathbed to come back and haunt John Bell and his descendants.

Seems she kept her promise. John Bell's torment began not long after Kate's death in 1817. The weirdness began with rapping sounds inside Bell's Adams, Tennessee, home. The rapping escalated, getting louder and stronger each night.

Next came the sound of rats gnawing at the children's bedposts, and soon the children were terrified by unseen hands yanking their blankets and pillows from the bed and throwing them to the floor. As time progressed, the Bells began hearing the sounds of whispers. The voices were too faint to be understood, but it sounded like an old woman singing hymns. Other things, such as sugar and milk being spilled on the table, occurred. And around this time, John and his oldest daughter, Betsy, became targets of Kate's wrath. She would pinch and scratch them, yank their hair, pull their noses, and poke needles into them. She would brutally slap Betsy, leaving red marks on her cheeks and body. Often the attacks were followed by gleeful, cackling laughter.

Bell at first tried to keep the ghost a secret, but word got out, and people began coming to see for themselves. Obviously pleased with the attention, Kate reportedly began talking, holding intelligent conversations with visitors. When content, her voice had a pleasing musical tone. However, when she was displeased, she spoke in a nerve-wracking shrill voice. Often, if she were happy with the company, she would sing hymns to entertain them.

The Bell Witch, as she came to be known, became quite famous. In 1819, word of her hauntings reached the ears of General Andrew Jackson, with whom John's sons, John Jr. and Jesse, had fought in the Battle of New Orleans. Curious, Jackson decided to take a road trip to check things out.

Journeying from Nashville, Jackson brought an entourage of several men and a large wagon. As the group approached the Bell property, the wagon came to a sudden halt and, despite the best efforts of the horses, would not be moved.

The men cursed and pushed and pushed and cursed, but the wagon remained still. After several minutes, Jackson commented that they must have encountered the Bell Witch. No sooner had the words left his mouth, than a disembodied female voice spoke up, telling the group that they could continue and that she would see them later on. They traveled on to the Bell home without further incident.

That night, Jackson and his men sat with John Bell, talking of Indians and politics, waiting for the Bell Witch to pipe in. They sat talking for hours, but no witch. Finally, one of Jackson's men claimed to be a witch tamer. He pulled a pistol and said he was going to call the witch up and kill her.

Immediately following his proclamation, the gentleman began screaming and squirming. He said there were needles being poked into his body. He ran from the house, saying that he was being beaten. The sound of cackling laughter followed him, though it's not certain if it was Kate doing the giggling or his buddies.

Jackson and his men left the next day. Later,

Jackson said, "I'd rather fight the entire British army than to deal with the Bell Witch."

Although John and Betsy were special targets of Kate's mischief, all members of the Bell family were victims. All, at one time or another, had been pinched; had been kicked; had been slapped; or had had their blankets pulled off in the middle of cold nights. Kate terrified them all. All, that is, except John Jr.

John Jr. wasn't afraid of Kate, and he let her know it. He cursed and yelled at her, a boldness that she found interesting. She often remarked on his intelligence, and the two spent much time in lively debates, conversations which were later included in *The Bell Witch—A Mysterious Spirit*, a book written by Charles Bailey Bell, John Jr.'s grandson. The book was published in 1934.

Kate may have liked John Jr., but for some reason, she took a particular dislike to Betsy Bell. For years, she had singled her out for abuse, slapping and kicking her until she was bruised and battered. In her twenties, Betsy fell in love with Joshua Gardner, a local young man. The two became engaged, but it wasn't the blissful event it should have been for Betsy, for Kate took a dislike to poor Joshua.

The witch's objections to Gardner were unknown, but she repeatedly told Betsy that she wouldn't be happy with him. She said Betsy should marry local schoolteacher Richard Powell instead. Reportedly a student of the occult, Powell had long been in love with Betsy. Many speculated that he was the force behind Kate.

Every time Betsy and Joshua were together, no matter where, Kate followed and harassed them terribly. She screamed. She hit. She taunted. The persecution built to a crescendo, and finally, the couple could take it no longer. On Easter Sunday 1821, Betsy and Joshua met at the river, and Betsy tearfully broke off the engagement.

It should be noted that Betsy did eventually marry Richard Powell, and by all reports had a happy life with him. So perhaps Miss Kate was right to break up the engagement to Joshua. Then again, maybe she, in her vindictiveness, was ticked off that things worked out for Betsy after all.

There is speculation that Kate carried her vindictiveness toward John to a murderous level. For several years, John Bell had battled a mysterious nervous system disorder that had gradually crippled

42

him. As his health deteriorated and he took to his bed, Kate would increase her harassment of him—slapping, screaming, pinching, anything to keep him from getting the healing rest he needed.

On December 20, 1820, John Bell died in his bed. Immediately upon finding him dead, his family discovered a small vial of dark liquid on the table next to his bed. Not knowing what it was, but suspicious, they gave a bit to the family cat. The poor kitty died almost instantly. That's when Kate piped in with her cackling laughter. "I gave ol' Jack a big dose of that last night, and that fixed him," she's quoted as saying. In a rage, John Jr. dashed the vial into the burning fireplace.

When you consider the symptoms Bell suffered—seizures, headaches, numbness, tingling sensations, and fatigue—and realize that these are the same symptoms someone would experience if they were being poisoned … Well, you just gotta wonder if Kate was sneaking a wee tad of that stuff into ol' John's coffee every morning for years.

Anyway, Kate was gleeful at Bell's death. As his body was being placed into the ground, she laughed and sang hymns. And it was all over a little neighborly dispute.

The incidents of Kate's shenanigans became fewer after Bell's death. Finally, in April of 1821, she visited John Jr. and told him that she would return to visit with him in seven years. She reportedly kept her word and returned in 1828, at which time the two engaged in scholarly conversations. They discussed the origin of life, Christianity, and other profound subjects. Significantly, it's reported that Kate told John Jr. of the coming of the Civil War, World War I, the Depression, and World War II.

Reportedly, after visiting for about three weeks, Kate said farewell to John Jr., telling him she would return to visit his closest descendant in 107 years. That descendant was grandson Charles Bailey Bell, a Nashville physician. Although Charles Bell wrote a book about the Bell Witch, it seems that Kate did not keep her promise to return. At least if she did return, she didn't talk with Charles.

Some believe she did return, however, and that, indeed, she's still around. These folks believe that the strange happenings centered around a cave located on the old John Bell property are Kate having a bit of fun. Ghostly figures have been seen wandering the area around the cave, and strange noises, such as voices whispering and weird knocking sounds, have been heard.

If you're looking for a spooky adventure, try a visit to the Bell Witch Cave. The current owners open it for tours by appointment. According to one of the owners, on several occasions she and the tourists have sighted strange apparitions and heard weird sounds coming from deep inside the cave.

But if you do visit, mind your P's & Q's. Kate's someone you don't want to tick off!

Ghostly Productions

Ghostly Productions

Theaters everywhere are notorious for being haunted. Tennessee's theaters are no exception. And since Tennessee is the Birthplace of Country Music, you just might come face to face with a star or two.

The Ryman Auditorium

The Ryman Auditorium is one of Tennessee's oldest buildings. Prominent Nashville riverboat captain Thomas Ryman built it in 1892 and called the building the Union Gospel Tabernacle.

The late 1800s were a boom time for Nashville, which became the cultural and commercial center for the post-Civil War South. Modernization of the city's rail center and river ports drew farmers, factories, and traders bringing their goods for trade. Nashville was a hustling, bustling, thriving metropolis.

A graduate of the school of hard knocks, Ryman could barely read or write, but he was a shrewd businessman. As a boy, he'd learned the river life

fishing with his dad. As a young man, he took that
knowledge and began a commercial fishing business.
During the Civil War, he made enough money selling
fish to both Union and Confederate troops to buy his
first steamboat.

By 1885, Ryman had thirty-five steamboats on the
Cumberland and Tennessee rivers and was one of the
most influential men in Nashville. He built a beautiful
mansion in one of the city's best neighborhoods and
was active in the politics of the city.

By all accounts, Ryman was a bit of a rounder who
loved to drink and party. In addition to his steamboats,
he owned a couple of saloons on Broad Street. He also
sold whiskey for a nickel a shot on his steamboats, and
liquor was one of his main cargos.

The partying came to an end, however, when
Ryman attended a religious revival. Cartersville,
Georgia, evangelist Sam Jones conducted the revival,
and it was a life-changing experience for the captain,
who converted to Christianity and became fervently
religious thereafter.

Ryman vowed to clean up Nashville, beginning
with his own businesses. According to legend, he left
the revival and immediately went to his saloons, where

he and some helpful friends took all the liquor and poured it into the Cumberland River. He then ridded his boats of liquor and never sold a drop of it again.

That contribution wasn't enough, however. He approached Jones with the idea to raise funds to build a tabernacle, a project that he threw his heart into and worked on tirelessly for ten years. The original building was completed and opened as the Union Gospel Tabernacle in 1892. Immediately, revivals were held here that brought people and business into Nashville.

In 1897, Nashville would celebrate its centennial, and the city fathers wanted a venue large enough to hold large conventions to coincide with this event. Jones and Ryman again raised money and added a gallery onto the tabernacle. In 1897, the Confederate Veterans held their convention in Nashville, with more than one hundred thousand members attending. The tabernacle served as their headquarters. The veterans were so impressed that they donated money to complete the tabernacle's balcony. In return, the balcony was named the Confederate Gallery.

The tabernacle became a popular place for conventions, shows, and other types of entertainment.

However, Ryman was adamant that all presentations be "moral" according to his Christian standards.

Ryman died in 1904 after a prolonged illness. His contributions to Nashville had been many, and he was recognized as a true father of the city. More than four thousand people packed into the auditorium to bid him farewell. Although he had refused to have his tabernacle named for him in life, after his death, it was renamed the Ryman Auditorium.

With Ryman no longer around to censor the content, the auditorium became a venue for popular entertainment. Recognized as having superior acoustics, it became a nationally known concert hall and stage. Prestigious presentations of *Carmen*, *The Barber of Seville*, and *Faust* drew the best and brightest to Nashville and helped to change the city's cultural history. Jenny Lind, Rudolph Valentino, Will Rogers, Mary Pickford, Charlie Chaplin, and Douglas Fairbanks were just a few of the cultural icons who performed here to audiences that often included celebrities such as Theodore and Eleanor Roosevelt, and Helen Keller.

At the same time the Ryman was gaining popularity as an entertainment venue, a live country music radio show called the *WSM Barn Dance* was also gaining an audience. Begun in 1925, the show became an international phenomenon, drawing in ever-growing crowds. The show moved several times over the years, but always outgrew its venue. Finally, in 1943, the *Grand Ole Opry* moved into the three thousand-seat Ryman Auditorium and began a relationship that lasted thirty-one years.

As the site of the *Grand Ole Opry* from 1943 until 1974, the stage of the Ryman hosted all the biggest country music artists: Hank Williams Jr., Roy Acuff, Jimmie Rodgers, The Carter Family, Patsy Cline, Johnny Cash, Elvis Presley, Dolly Parton, and so many more.

The Ryman was closed when the *Opry* moved, and it stayed empty, slowly deteriorating, until 1994, when a group of concerned citizens and businessmen decided it needed to be saved. It was restored and reopened as a theater of national fame.

Today, it's recognized as one of the best concert halls in the nation, with close to perfect acoustics. Although the world's biggest stars from every music genre come here to play, the Ryman Auditorium remains the country music mecca. As new performers step onto that stage for the first time, they can't help but hear the echo of those other voices, the ones that sing to them from a hallowed past.

The Ghosts of the Ryman

Like other storied theaters around the world, the Ryman Auditorium is haunted by a host of spirits. The first to be identified was the ghost of Thomas Ryman. According to the ghostly legend, Ryman first appeared not long after his death. He made that first appearance during the performance of a stage show with a rather risqué content.

Reportedly, he made so much noise that patrons complained of not being able to hear the show. He's also made appearances during many others shows that, considering his religious background, he would have considered unacceptable. Each time he makes enough noise that it's impossible to follow the show.

During the 1960s, when the *Grand Ole Opry* was in its heyday and other shows, such as *The Jimmie Dean Show*, were recorded here, artists and production crews came from all over the country to perform and record here.

During the taping of one show, a production crew

from New York had been talking with a local crew, who told them about the ghost of Thomas Ryman. Well, of course, this crew just thought it was a joke that the local yokels were trying to get one over on the big city fellas. They laughed and said they'd call the bluff. They agreed to hang around the theater that night to prove there were no spirits wandering the theater.

Things were quiet until the stroke of midnight. Suddenly, they began hearing the sound of heavy footsteps echoing through the theater. With each step, dust floated down from between the edges of the ceiling tiles beneath the gallery. Startled, they checked the theater. Except for them, it was empty. The crew packed up its gear and returned posthaste to the big city.

Another spirit that makes regular appearances in the Ryman is the Gray Man, so called because of the gray suit he wears. This mysterious entity never appears during performances. He prefers instead to show himself to maintenance or cleanup crews in the theater's after hours. He's also been known to show up for a rehearsal every now and again.

The Gray Man is always spotted sitting quietly in

the balcony. If someone goes up to send him away, they find the balcony deserted. Then when they return downstairs and look back up, he's once again seated in the balcony. No one knows who the Gray Man is or why he haunts the Ryman, but those who've seen him know he exists.

There's a third spirit that haunts the Ryman, but he's got no problem being recognized. Reportedly, the spirit of Hank Williams Sr. still treads the boards of Ryman's historic stage. Williams began making appearances not long after his death in an automobile accident in 1953. On one Saturday afternoon, country music artist "Whispering" Bill Anderson was on the Ryman stage rehearsing for the evening show. At one point, he began strumming a song that was reputed to be a personal favorite of Williams. Suddenly, everything went dead—the house lights, the sound system, everything. No reason was ever found for the shutdown, and Anderson remarked that he thought the eerie experience was somehow related to the Hank Williams Sr. song.

An even eerier incident happened to a construction worker when the auditorium was being restored in the 1990s. The poor fellow got locked in the empty theater one late night. The worker said as he was walking through the theater sometime during that night, he turned a corner and came face to face with Hank Williams Sr. As he stood there, Hank just faded away.

That's what old ghosts do, isn't it? Just fade away?

The Bijou Theater

Since the time it was built in 1817, the building that now houses the Bijou Theater has served as a social hub for Knoxville. It was to begin life as a hotel and tavern named the Thomas Humes House, after its exceedingly modest builder. Humes, however, died shortly before construction was completed, and the building was rented out to another modest fellow, who called the place Archie Ray's Tavern. He later renamed it the Knoxville House.

The Knoxville House had thirteen rooms, a bar, a ballroom, and a dining room. It became a popular meeting spot and hosted many social gatherings and entertained such VIPs as General Andrew Jackson.

When his lease was up in 1821, Ray did not renew, and little is known about the hotel until 1823, when it once again became the hub of social life in Knoxville under the management of a General Joseph Jackson, who owned it for thirteen years. He sold it in 1836 to James Pickett.

Pickett remodeled and named it the City Hotel, but in 1842, the poor man found himself unable to pay his bills. He had to sell the hotel. It changed hands several times, then in 1852, a Yankee businessman named Coleman bought it, and renamed the hotel the Coleman House. He also expanded the hotel, practically doubling its previous size. A new kitchen, an elevator, parlors, a dining room, a courtyard, a ladies' entrance, and a new ballroom were added.

In 1857, the hotel was bought by Knoxville businessman William Sneed, who renamed it the Lamar House in honor of New York banker Gazaway Bugg Lamar. Lamar had invested a large sum of money in the development of Knoxville.

The Lamar House was an important part of Knoxville's social scene until the Civil War broke out. Sneed, a Confederate sympathizer, fled town when the Union marched in and took over. The Yankees commandeered the Lamar House and turned part of it into a hospital, known as (what else?) the Lamar Hospital.

Union generals Sherman and Sheridan made the Lamar Hospital their headquarters, poring over their battle plans laid out on the dining room table. On November 17, 1863, Brigadier General William Sanders was mortally wounded in battle. He was brought to the hospital and placed in the old bridal suite, where, after a night in agony, he died.

After the war, Sneed returned and sued the government to retrieve the hotel, and once again, the good times rolled. In 1877, Rutherford B. Hayes visited and gave a rousing speech from the hotel's balcony, and the hotel threw him a big party.

The good times rolled right on into the 1890s, with visits from local, national, and international celebrities. There were also so many presidential visits—both from the past and in those current times—that by 1895, the place was renamed The White House.

Ah, but good times can't go on forever. In 1900, the hotel was auctioned off for a mere $25. It was known as the new LaMarr House in 1903-1904, and then as the Homestead from 1904 until 1907. The hotel's owner then sold it to the Auditorium Company, turning his $25 investment into a $50,000 profit.

Deciding it was time for a change, the company's investors remodeled, turning a large portion of the hotel into a theater called Jake Wells's Bijou Theater. The back portion of the building remained a hotel with a separate entrance and became a separate entity. The Bijou opened in 1909. Its first production starred George M. Cohan in *Little Johnny Jones*.

As an owner of thirty theaters, Jake Wells had experience in running a theater, and soon the Bijou was proclaimed as one of the South's finest. That didn't last long. The theater and hotel changed management several times, and the ensuing years were not kind.

Like an aging Southern belle with a tattered petticoat and too much rouge, the hotel took on a tired look—a little ragged around the edges, but holding on to an air of dignity. By 1957, however, "worn" no longer fit. The word now was "seedy." Maybe even downright "sleazy."

The grand old hotel, once again known as the LaMarr House, had degenerated into the hangout of transients and prostitutes. It continued to deteriorate until 1969, when a public outcry prompted a circuit judge to order the place closed. It had been in operation for 152 years.

The Bijou fared little better, although it enjoyed a heyday of almost twenty years. In 1913, it became a vaudeville theater, with an occasional movie being shown. Notable acts that performed here include the Marx Brothers, Blackstone the Magician, and John Philip Sousa and his band. An old fire door in the theater's fly space contains the signatures of the vaudeville acts that performed the last show at the Bijou.

In 1926, the builders of the Tennessee Theater bought it, but not because they wanted to continue running it as a theater. That would be competition. Instead, they sold the property to a Knoxville businessman with the stipulation that it not be used for any theatrical productions for five years.

The Bijou spent time as a used car lot, and its entrance was the Bijou Fruit Stand, where Knoxville's first banana was sold. In 1932, it was reopened as the LaConte Hotel, with rooms for one dollar.

In 1935, a division of Paramount Pictures leased the building for thirty years, where they screened second-run movies that had already been shown at the Tennessee. In addition, the theater also occasionally featured plays. Tallulah Bankhead appeared in *Little*

Foxes, and Ethel Barrymore appeared in *The Corn is Green* during this time.

After Paramount's lease expired, the theater was renamed the Bijou Art Theater and was leased to a company that showed "adult" films, which caused another of those public outcries. The property, however, had come into the hands of the Rasnakes of Knoxville. At the death of Mrs. Rasnakes, it was donated to the United Methodist Church.

That'd be a turnaround, wouldn't you think? Not so. Records show that from 1971 until 1973, the theater featured exotic dancers, novelty acts, and burlesque shows. Finally in 1973, it was closed down because of unpaid rent and was scheduled for demolition.

Fortunately, the good folks of Knoxville recognized the historical value of the building and a rescue was performed. Through donations and fundraisers, the building was bought and restored. Today, the Bijou Theater, its dignity restored, is one of Knoxville's most prominent performance venues.

The Ghosts of the Bijou

The spirit of an unidentified man is one of the ghosts haunting the Bijou. No one knows for sure who he is, but considering how many different owners this theater has had, my money is on a former owner still taking care of things. Or perhaps it's Smiley, a former employee who's believed to still be here.

There have been so many reports of ghosts in the Bijou, that a local ghost-hunting organization was invited to conduct an investigation there. Though no actual sightings were made, the group did encounter some pretty spooky things, including hearing knocking sounds and banging throughout their investigation. Several members heard the sound of coins being dropped on one of the stairways. While exploring up on the fourth floor, one of the members decided to try to call up Smiley. She called his name and instantly felt as if someone was standing behind her. She also felt a brush of air on her neck and heard a sigh.

One brave member stayed after everyone had left. She said the whole time she was spreading out a pallet of blankets, she felt an icy cold finger poking her in the side. She ignored it and climbed into her makeshift bed. Moments later, she felt the blanket beside her being pushed down, and she looked at the pillow next to her to see a depression in it, as if a head were pillowed there.

Still she stayed. She even managed to fall asleep and reported hearing the sounds of a vacuum cleaner running for about fifteen minutes—though no cleaning crew was there.

Photos were taken throughout the theater, and many "orbs"—points of light that are reportedly the manifestation of spirits—were captured. The team also reported capturing a photo of a bearded man wearing white suspenders. He was seated in the theater's balcony.

The investigators concluded that there definitely was spirit activity in the Bijou Theater and that further investigation was warranted. I've concluded that those folks are a lot braver than I am.

The Orpheum Theater

The Orpheum Theater opened in 1890 as the Grand Opera House. And it was grand. Located on the corner of Memphis's Main and Beale streets, it was known as the "South's Finest Theater."

The theater was originally used for opera, but let's

face it, ya gotta bring in the folks, and opera just doesn't pack 'em in. Pretty soon, the Grand was featuring vaudeville acts, and in 1907, it became a part of the Orpheum Circuit, a prestigious theater company, with venues throughout the country. The name was changed that year.

Vaudeville was a successful venture for the Orpheum for more than twenty years. But in 1923, a fire broke out during a show featuring striptease artist Blossom Seeley. The original building burned down to the foundation.

It sat for five long years before rising from the ashes, a beautiful phoenix, twice as large and even more luxurious than before. The builders spent a whopping $1.5 million—unheard of in that time—to reconstruct the Orpheum. Decorated in the style of François I (whoever that is), the theater sported an enormous domed ceiling, twin staircases in the grand lobby, giant crystal chandeliers, and gilded plasterwork. A Mighty Wurlitzer organ provided music from the orchestra pit. The auditorium seated almost three thousand, and was decorated in rich tones of gold, red, and cream. There was even a nightclub, called the Broadway Club, located within the theater.

By the 1940s, vaudeville had died and the Orpheum began floundering. It was sold to a movie company and began showing first run movies, which it did until 1977, when it closed. Again it languished for five years, until the Memphis Development Foundation acquired it and completed a $5 million renovation that restored the theater to its 1920s glory.

Today, the Orpheum is Memphis's premier Broadway venue. It has hosted more Broadway productions than any other theater in the country. In addition, the Orpheum hosts concerts featuring everyone from the Vienna Boys Choir to Sheryl Crow, and selected movies during the season.

Spirits of the Orpheum

There is one main spirit that haunts the Orpheum. She's a young girl, whom patrons have named Mary. Details about the little girl are sketchy, but reportedly, she's the spirit of a little girl who was struck and killed by a car on Beale Street. Somehow she found her way into the Orpheum and decided to stay. She's been appearing here for more than sixty years.

Witnesses say that she opens and closes doors and can be heard giggling sometimes. Throughout the years, patrons have reported seeing her sitting in seat C-5, which seems to be her favorite one. She reportedly sits very quietly and never makes a disturbance.

She has a mischievous streak, often pulling pranks on employees and others. Back in 1977, the traveling cast of the Broadway show *Fiddler on the Roof* had so many mysterious experiences here that they insisted on conducting a séance on the upper balcony, in hopes of contacting the offending spirit. Mary, however, chose not to appear.

A parapsychology class from the University of Memphis had better luck. In 1979, they conducted an investigation and found that Mary may not be the only spirit living in the Orpheum. She may well have chosen the theater because it was a place where she wouldn't be alone. The class, in fact, found the Orpheum to be well populated, spiritually speaking. By the time they left, they said they had found evidence of at least six other ghosts living here.

Who are these spirits? No one knows. It should be no wonder, however, that they've chosen to hang out for a time in the Orpheum. The theater is a huge part of Memphis history, and for generations, it's played an important role in the history of Memphisans. Ask anyone who grew up here, and, no doubt, they'll tell you of the time … their grandmother took them to see *42nd Street*; they had their first real date here; they stole their first kiss in the theater balcony.

The Orpheum has been a happy place for many people. It's full of so many fond memories. Why not think that some spirits might find their way back here? And, besides, if you were a ghost, where would you rather hang out? In some dark and dank mansion or cemetery? Nah. Bet you'd prefer a place full of lights, of action, of life.

The Missing Monk

The Missing Monk

"What a wonderful stroke of luck has fallen into my path," thought the doctor, as he picked himself up from the muddy ground. Hours before, he had been awakened by the sound of crunching, screeching metal, and human screams of terror. He knew instantly what had happened.

The heavy rains that day had whipped the normally gentle Hiawassee River into a roiling flood of white-water destruction. He'd feared that the waters would keep rising and break free of its banks, washing away everything in its path. And the railroad tracks were in its path.

He'd known as soon as he heard the squealing brakes and the crashing metal that the flood waters had, indeed, breached its banks. It had washed out a section of the tracks. And he knew that what he'd just heard was the Norfolk Southern, filled with passengers, plunging into the ravine.

The next hours had been a blur of non-stop activity. A rescue party had been dispatched from

Charleston, and within minutes they had begun pulling the injured—and the dead—from the wreckage. There was no morgue, so the dead, dozens of them, were stacked in the railroad depot.

There also was no hospital, so the injured had been taken to private homes, and he had traveled from home to home, treating everything from cut heads to traumatic amputations. It had been a horrible night of blood and death, and he was close to collapse from physical exhaustion.

All he'd been thinking about was getting to his home, cleaning up, and catching a nap before daylight dawned. But then he'd stumbled over something in his path and landed on his rear in the mud. When he figured out just what he'd tripped over, he was delighted despite his exhaustion. This was something he'd wanted for quite a long time. He'd just never figured out a way to get it. And now, here it'd just fallen right into his path.

He raised his lantern and looked down. It seemed to be just the right size for what he had in mind, not too big. It wouldn't be too hard to process, he was sure. He pulled it up on his shoulder, staggering under the weight. He had to hurry before anyone saw him.

Luckily, he wasn't far from his house, which also served as his medical office. He staggered into a room, and deposited his find onto the table. Finally, able to get a good look at it, he was startled to see a brown monk's brown habit and rosary beads. Not that it really mattered—he was a man of science, not religion. The fact that the man lying on the table had been a man of God didn't change his plans in any way.

Leaving the body on the table, he went out into his backyard. There was a huge cauldron there. He'd been told the previous owners used it to prepare hogs after slaughter. He smiled to himself. It was serendipity, he supposed, that it was here in his backyard. It was perfect for what he had in mind.

First, he started a fire underneath the pot, then began filling it with water, an endeavor that took some time. He'd get cleaned up, he decided, and then prepare the monk's body. He was dead tired, but he had to get this done before daylight. The town was sleeping, with everyone exhausted from the night's excitement. There wouldn't be a better time.

After he'd cleaned up, he returned to the examining room. Removing the habit and underclothes from the body was difficult, but he got it done. He

then took a moment to look over the body. The eyes
were open and staring straight at him, sending a
sudden chill through him. Surprised at such a
reaction, he tried to shake it off. As a physician, he'd
seen that death look many times. Sometimes it
saddened him, but it had never frightened him. He
tried to close the eyes, but rigor had set in, and the
lids wouldn't be moved.

Continuing his examination, he briefly noted that
the monk had been a handsome man. No doubt, his
decision to become a priest had disappointed many
would-be lovers. In keeping with this life of discipline
and self-denial, he was slim and looked to be fit.

The cause of death was obvious when his
examination reached the lower body. An ugly gash
across the upper thigh had, no doubt, cut the femoral
artery. He had probably struggled from the wreckage
and was trying to reach help when he collapsed from
loss of blood. With darkness hiding him, he had
simply bled to death where he fell.

Checking the cauldron, the doctor found the water
beginning to bubble. He returned to the room,
shouldered the monk's body, and carried him out to
the backyard. Getting him into the cauldron wasn't

difficult, but getting his body completely underwater was a problem. He had to bend the monk double and push hard. Still there were parts of the back that were out of the water. He'd have to turn him over to be sure all the skin was boiled.

As the water bubbled around the body, an aroma of cooking flesh began to permeate the air. It smelled as if someone were cooking a roast. The doctor worried that his neighbors would be curious, but everyone seemed to still be sleeping. After a while, he used a large stick he'd found in his yard to flip the body. While he was waiting, he dug a hole in his garden. So focused was he on his task that the ghoulishness of his actions never once crossed his mind. The man was dead, he had already reasoned. What did it matter?

As he was waiting, the doctor went back into the house and gathered up the monk's habit and rosary. He hung them inside a small space hidden underneath the attic stairs. Later, he would board over the area so no one would notice it.

Finished with that task, he hurried back outside and once again checked the body in the cauldron. Perfect. Flesh was falling from the bone. He grabbed a knife and began cutting away the stubborn parts, leaving, however, the tendons that held the bones together.

It was a gruesome task, and at times the doctor found himself gagging. But it had to be done. He'd come this far. No turning back now. After the bones were as clean as he could get them, he carried the skeleton into the house and returned to empty the cauldron. But there was no time to let it cool. He had to bury the flesh before daylight.

As he shoveled the meat into the hole he'd dug, he heard a sound behind him. His heart in his throat, he turned to find the neighbor's dog sitting there, looking up at him with expectant eyes. Relief flooded him. Smiling, he tossed the dog a morsel.

Sitting in his office later, a whiskey clutched in his hand, he finally allowed himself to relax. Small pieces of flesh still clung to the bones, but a couple of weeks in a vat of bleach and that would all be gone. The bones would be clean and white, and he'd have a skeleton to hang in his office.

That corner right there, he thought, will be perfect. Then, he'd have something he could use as a reference with his patients with broken bones. He could show them exactly which bone was broken. It would be educational. When you thought about it, you could just consider that the monk's body had been donated to science.

No one would ever know. And it was free. Medical supplies had gotten so expensive, and he was just a small town doctor. Most of the time he was paid in vegetables or chickens. How was he supposed to buy supplies with that?

He rose and carefully picked up the skeleton, carrying it draped over his arms as if carrying a child. He'd take it to the attic, where there was a vat large enough. The bleach would keep the flesh from smelling.

In the days that followed the train wreck, there was an extensive search for the missing monk, who, the doctor learned from searchers, had been from Baltimore. His disappearance was a mystery, for all other passengers had been accounted for. Dozens had lost their lives in the tragedy, and dozens more had been seriously injured. But everyone else had been located. After a week, the search was called off and the monk's whereabouts remained a mystery.

The doctor waited one month. By that time, the furor over the wreck and the monk's disappearance had dissipated. He felt safe in unveiling his new prize. He'd drilled a hole in the top of the skull and placed a hook in it so that he could hang the skeleton on a movable frame. It was in the corner of his office right now. Looked nice, he thought. Not your typical decorator piece, but appropriate for a doctor's office.

It wasn't until several weeks later that the doctor began to rethink his decorating ideas. It started with terrible nightmares, in which he dreamed about the night he'd found the dead monk. In the dream, when he began to put the body into the cauldron of boiling water, the monk began to scream. It was a terrible, pain-filled scream that pierced the night and echoed in his ears even after he'd jerked awake with a scream of his own.

The nightmares were only a precursor to what was to follow. One night, after he'd awakened from the same nightmare, his heart pounding in his chest, he was frightened to see a dark figure standing beside his bed. He strained his eye in the darkness. The figure seemed to be wearing a long robe of some kind, with a hood pulled over the head. The arms were folded, with its hands disappearing into the sleeves of the robe. A rosary hung from the figure's waist.

The doctor blinked. He must still be dreaming. There was no way that someone wearing a monk's robe would be standing beside his bed. Was someone pulling a prank on him? He knew a few people in town were suspect of his new skeleton. There had been whispers, but, of course, no one could prove anything.

"Who are you?" he quavered.

There was no answer, but the figure reached up and pushed the cowl from his head, revealing his face. The doctor let out a squeak. It was the face of the monk, staring at him with those dead eyes. The doctor pinched himself, just to be sure he was awake. He was.

"Wwh-what do you want?" he asked. There was no answer, but suddenly the fully fleshed monk disappeared, and in his place was the skeleton, still wearing the monk's robe. Darkness filled the eyeless holes, but the teeth gleamed at him in a rictus grin.

"Tell me what you want!"

The skeleton stood there next to the bed silently for several more seconds, then faded away. The doctor collapsed back onto his pillow. His heart was pounding, and he was almost hyperventilating. He was soaked in a cold sweat. "I hope that never happens again!" he thought.

The good doctor didn't get his wish. Reportedly, the phantom monk appeared to him quite often. And, he continued to appear long after the doctor was gone. The next occupant of the building, Dr. J. Lake McClary, encountered the spirit on many occasions during his time there. He'd heard the rumors about the doctor and his skeleton. So he had a good idea about who the spirit was.

In 1932, when the building was demolished, workers made a discovery that seemed to confirm all suspicions of the doctor. Hanging in a small space between the walls, they found a monk's habit and rosary.

Today, the Coon Hunter's Association building stands near the site of the old doctor's office. Charleston residents have reported sometimes seeing the monk wandering down by the railroad tracks or near the Coon Hunter's building. Sensing an unhappiness emanating from him, they say they hope he someday finds peace.

The Bloody Mausoleum

The Bloody Mausoleum

Cleveland, Tennessee, is the site of one of those phenomena that can't be explained by logic. What has caused the mysterious blood-like stains on the Craigmiles' family mausoleum? Could it be the tragedy of a family that lost so many members to violent deaths? Or is it just the effects of weathering on the mausoleum's granite?

John Henderson Craigmiles was a Cleveland mercantile businessman in the 1850s. His business was successful, but Craigmiles wasn't satisfied. It just wasn't enough. He was restless. A little adventure was in order, he thought.

Leaving the business in his brother's hands, he headed out to California to seek his fortune in the gold rush. It didn't take him long to realize that the life of a gold panner wasn't for him.

He did strike it rich, though not by panning for gold. After being there for only a few weeks, Craigmiles discovered that someone with a little business sense

82

could make a lot of money by supplying the needs of the western territory.

He bought a fleet of six ships and began a shipping line between California and Panama. Not only could he trade between Central America and the West Coast, he could carry passengers as well. Things went really well, and Craigmiles made a lot of money. Then, disaster struck. Five of his fully loaded ships were hijacked by mutinous crew members. Claims from his creditors financially wiped out Craigmiles.

He wasn't down long, however. With a $600 stake borrowed from his brother, he rebuilt his business with the ship he had left. By 1857, he'd made another fortune and returned to Cleveland, Tennessee, to settle down.

Soon after he returned, Craigmiles fell in love with Adelia Thompson, daughter of Gideon Thompson, the town doctor. Not long after they married, the Civil War began. Craigmiles, because of his shipping and supply experience, was appointed chief commissary agent for the South, a position he held throughout the war. Reportedly, Craigmiles used the position to his advantage, buying cattle and speculating in cotton. He made a fortune off the war and, wise enough to know paper money was of little value, he traded only in

83

gold. When the war was over and Confederate money was worthless, Craigmiles still had his gold.

In 1864, John and Adelia had a daughter, whom they named Nina. John was completely devoted to his daughter, and, indeed, she was doted on by the entire family. Her grandfather, Dr. Thompson, liked nothing better than spending time with the little girl. When she was old enough, he would take her for walks and buggy rides around town. He even took her on medical calls with him every now and then. It was on one of their daily outings that tragedy struck.

Thompson and Nina were riding in a carriage on October 18, 1871, when Thompson somehow lost control of the horses. The carriage careened in front of an approaching train. Thompson was thrown clear, but Nina was still in the carriage when it hit the train. She was killed instantly.

The entire family was devastated by the little girl's death. Indeed, the entire town mourned her loss. Understandably, the family was barely able to get through the funeral.

After her funeral, Craigmiles wanted to do something in her memory. Since the Episcopal congregation where he attended services had no permanent meeting place, he decided that a new church would be a fitting honor. St. Luke's Episcopal Church was finished on October 18, 1874, the third anniversary of her death.

Adjacent to the church, Craigmiles also had a family mausoleum built. Constructed with expensive marble with four-foot-thick walls, it rose more than thirty-seven feet high, and was topped by a cross at the marble spire. Inside, the mausoleum contained six shelves for the Craigmiles family. When it was complete, Nina's body was disinterred and was placed into a special marble sarcophagus.

Not long after Nina was re-interred, people began to notice strange stains on the top of the mausoleum arch. They looked like bloodstains, and no matter how much they were scrubbed, they just wouldn't go away.

Soon after, an infant son born to John and Adelia died only hours after birth and was interred inside the mausoleum next to his sister. In 1899, John Craigmiles died. He had slipped and fallen in the street one day and developed an infection that turned into blood poisoning. He was placed in the mausoleum along with his children.

Then, in 1928, Adelia was killed when a car struck

her she while she was crossing the street. She was laid to rest with her family in the mausoleum.

Reports are that as each family member was placed into the mausoleum, the mysterious stains became larger and more numerous. Workmen tried to clean them off, but they remained. Finally, in exasperation, the marble bearing the stains was removed and replaced with new, clean marble.

Several days later, the workmen found something that disconcerted them. When they checked the mausoleum marble, the stains had returned in the same spot as before. The process was repeated, with the stained marble removed and replaced with clean marble. And once again, the stains reappeared in just days.

According to many locals, the stains are bloodstains, oozing from the marble in response to the tragic deaths of the Craigmiles family. The stains remain today, one of life's unexplained mysteries.

Tennessee's Haunted Mansions

Tennessee's Haunted Mansions

Many of Tennessee's historic homes, some nearly two hundred years old, have been restored to their original beauty. Tour them, and you'll take a stroll down wisteria-scented lanes into Tennessee's history, to a time of antebellum homes, big dresses and corsets, and men on powerful steeds. Revolutionary and Civil War battles were fought on the lawns—and sometimes on the front steps—of these homes. Generations of families lived, loved, and died within their walls.

If you accept the possibility of ghosts, then you have to believe that Tennessee's historic homes are haunted places.

The Carter House, the Carnton Plantation, and the Battle of Franklin

These two historic homes are located just miles from each other. Both played a huge role in the Battle of Franklin, a Civil War battle that haunts both houses to this day.

The Battle of Franklin has been called "The

Gettysburg of the West." A bloody five-hour battle, it claimed more Confederate Army of Tennessee soldiers than the two-day Battle of Shiloh and the three-day Battle of Stones River.

It all began with the hubris of Confederate General John Hood, whose Tennessee Campaign of 1864 was designed to drive the Union out of Nashville and draw Sherman out of Atlanta. The Union army arrived in Franklin around 1:00 a.m. on November 30, 1864. They commandeered the Carter family home as their headquarters and began making plans for battle.

The Confederates arrived later that day, with Hood commanding. Posting just outside Franklin, he made plans for a frontal assault. His generals strongly objected. They knew the Union Army would be entrenched behind breastworks left from a battle the year before. A frontal attack, they said, would be suicidal. But Hood was insistent. Perhaps his ego was still stinging from the battle he had lost at nearby Spring Hill the day before. As it turns out, Hood should have heeded the advice of his generals.

The battle didn't begin until 4:00 p.m., with most of the fighting done after dark. The Confederates charged the breastworks with a wave of forces that forced the Union out, backing them up into the yard of the Carter house. Blue and gray uniforms intermingled in savage hand-to-hand combat that made it difficult for defending Union forces to fire upon approaching lines.

The combat took place in the front yard of the Carter house, with soldiers being bayoneted and beaten on the front steps and inside the house. Over and over, the Confederates smashed headlong into the Union line, with twenty thousand troops marching into direct fire and conducting seventeen assaults lasting more than five hours. Remarkably, they did route the Yankees, but the cost to the Rebel army was so great, it was hard to see the battle as a victory.

The Battle of Franklin devastated the Army of Tennessee, all but destroying it. There were 6,252 casualties, including fifteen generals, with six killed and the rest wounded or captured. Of the field grade officers, sixty-five were lost.

The Carter House

When the Union Army arrived in the wee hours of the morning, the Carter family, roused from their beds, took refuge in the basement and listened throughout the next night as the battle raged around them.

They heard gunfire, the sound of bullets hitting their home, and the screams of dying men. Battle was waged on the porch and throughout the rooms of the house. Soldiers were killed on the front steps and clubbed to death in the yard.

The smoke from canons and guns was so thick, it was hard to tell just whom to shoot, as time after time Confederates charged the Union position, only to be repulsed every time.

After the battle, the Carters climbed from the basement to the carnage of "the bloodiest hours of the American Civil War." More than twenty-five hundred Union soldiers were killed. Included in the Confederate casualties was the Carter's son Theodric (Tod). Found on the battlefield mortally wounded, he was brought to a first-floor bedroom, where he died.

Restored and opened to the public in 1953, the Carter House has the ignominious distinction of being the most battle-damaged building in the Civil War, with more than thirty-five hundred bullet holes still pock-marking the exterior. Today a Registered Historic Landmark, it operates as a museum and serves as a memorial to the Carter family and the thousands of soldiers who died there.

Considering all the death and carnage that occurred here, it's no wonder the place is haunted. There have been sightings of men in Civil War uniforms both in the yard and in the house, where some were killed in hand-to-hand combat.

Tod Carter has been sighted several times as well, most often in the first-floor bedroom where he died. Guests or staff members have peeked in to see him sitting on the side of the bed. He stays for only seconds before fading away.

By far the most active spirit is reported to be that of Tod's little sister, Annie. During a tour one day, tour members pointed out to a staff member that the statue behind her was jumping up and down—for no apparent reason. By all accounts, Annie is a playful little poltergeist, often tugging at sleeves and making objects disappear and reappear. One staff member claimed to have seen the apparition of a little girl running down a hallway.

Carnton Plantation

Built in 1824, the Carnton Plantation is a two-story, twenty-two-room mansion with white columns and front porches on both stories—the quintessential Southern plantation home. Its builder, Randall McGavock, built it to raise thoroughbred horses and various produce crops. It, too, has been turned into a museum. Located in Franklin, it is only a few miles from the Carter House, and although it wasn't in the thick of the fighting, it played an important role in the Battle of Franklin.

When Carrie McGavock, the second generation mistress of the house, began hearing guns and canon fire, and the screams of dying men late in the afternoon, she knew a battle was going on nearby. Night fell, but the fighting continued until after midnight, when rain and sleet began to fall and finally put an end to it all.

As wounded men gathered near Carnton, Carrie ordered the servants to roll up the carpets and to help the wounded inside. More than two hundred wounded soldiers were brought inside, where Carrie and her servants, and her two children, Hattie (nine) and Winder (seven), tore up clothing for bandages.

93

When physicians arrived, the children's bedroom was set up as an operating room, and Carrie and the children assisted in caring for the wounded. Several hundred soldiers were treated there that night, and more than 150 died. Bloodstains are still visible in many bedrooms, most notably in the children's room.

The dead were carried out to the back of the house. The bodies of four of the Army of Tennessee's most important generals were brought here. Reportedly, there were so many dead soldiers that the bodies had to be stood erect, side by side. Carrie recorded information about the dead, preserving names, initials, or just items that the men carried, in hopes of comforting their grieving families. Days later, the Confederate Army buried hundreds of soldiers outside the nearby Carter House.

However, in 1866, John McGavock saw that the graves were deteriorating. He set aside two acres of Carnton Plantation for the country's largest privately owned Confederate cemetery. Fifteen hundred bodies were re-interred here, in order by state. Carrie's meticulous burial records were used to place markers over the soldiers that were known. John and Carrie maintained the cemetery for the rest of their lives.

94

Carnton Mansion has been called "the most haunted building in Tennessee." Ghost stories abound. The most well-known ghost is that of the restless soldier who wanders through the house and across the back porch. He's also been seen walking through the yard. The sound of his heavy boots accompanies each sighting.

The Battle of Franklin wasn't the only death Carnton Plantation has known. According to legend, in the 1840s, a young house servant rejected the advances of a field hand. In a jealous rage, he caught her in the kitchen and killed her. It's believed the spirit of this young woman is one of two ghosts who haunts the kitchen. Sometimes the sound of dishes being washed can be heard, and mischievous tricks, such as moving objects around, are played on staff members.

There are frightening reports that the head of a Carnton cook has been seen floating down a hallway. No word on what happened to the rest of the body, but it must still be in the kitchen, for often there are sounds of cooking going on, and the aroma of food being cooked emanates throughout the building. She is usually heard around mealtimes.

A beautiful young woman with brown hair was

once sighted ascending the stairway. She so frightened the workman who was descending the stairs that he fled hurriedly. Afterward, the workmen insisted on working in pairs in the upstairs.

The spirit of a Confederate soldier haunts one of the home's bedrooms. Besides being seen, he also moved objects to make himself known. In one incident, a picture of the house crashed to the floor. When staff members investigated, they found it placed on top of a floor heater, where it could not have fallen by itself.

A lady in white has been seen on the back porch and sometimes floating into the backyard. It's thought that this is the gentle spirit of former mistress Carrie McGavock, still caring for her home—and perhaps the restless spirits of the Confederate soldiers who died here.

Confederate General Patrick Cleburne has been seen frequently, especially in the deepening dusk of fall evenings. In one truly remarkable incident, he appeared to a gentleman who had mistakenly come to the plantation on a day it was closed. As the visitor stood on the porch looking around, he saw a soldier dressed in a Confederate uniform about to mount a horse, but suddenly the horse disappeared. When he turned in surprise, he found another soldier dressed in gray standing next to him. Thinking a battle reenactment must be planned, he asked the soldier what happened to the horse.

The horse had been shot out from under the soldier, just as his own horse had been, was the reply. The soldier went on to say that the night's battle was going to be a massacre, whether on horse or afoot, and it was all the fault of that fool Hood. The soldier, who was dressed in an officer's uniform, asked the man where his gun was. When the man replied that he did he not have one, the soldier became concerned and told him to get himself to the Carter House or into town out of harm's way. The soldier then turned to an invisible companion and said, "Well, Gavon, if we're going to die, let's die like men." Throwing his hat angrily into the air, he disappeared.

The man then heard the sounds of battle, guns firing, orders being screamed, men dying, and a whole army of Rebel yells. Thoroughly frightened, he hurried out to his car, the din of battle surrounding him. A cold darkness seemed to weigh on his shoulders and he became confused, wandering around the Carnton graveyard for some time before locating his car and driving off.

The next day, the man returned to Carnton when it was open. Describing his experience to the staff, he discovered that the officer he had been talking to was none other than Confederate General Patrick Cleburne. Cleburne had been one of Hood's generals who strenuously objected to engaging the Union Army at Franklin, believing, rightly so, that it would be a slaughter.

Falcon Manor

Clay Faulkner was a forward thinking man. And a persuasive one. In 1896, the wealthy manufacturer made his wife a promise. As the manufacturer of Gorilla Pants, "pants so strong even a gorilla couldn't tear them apart," Faulkner wanted to be closer to his factory two and one-half miles outside of McMinnville.

Mary Faulkner, however, wasn't a big fan of the country life. Faulkner promised her that if she agreed to move to the country, he would build her the finest home in the county. She agreed. And he did.

Falcon Rest was the fulfillment of Faulkner's

promise. He meticulously supervised the building of the ten thousand-foot Victorian-style mansion. Insisting on only the finest materials and craftsmanship, he constructed a solid brick home, with interior and exterior brick walls built directly into the bedrock.

Instead of the gaudy ornate decorations favored in late 1800s construction, Faulkner chose graceful design elements for his home. Curved windows, a gingerbread porch, intricately carved woodwork, and a distinctive frieze in the parlor reflected an elegance not often seen in small town Tennessee.

Elegance intertwined with function in Faulkner's Falcon Rest. The house was positioned so that a breeze blew over its porches, even on the hottest days. A waterworks system from the cold waters of nearby Faulkner Springs provided refrigeration, water for cooking and bathing, and even cooling in the hot summers.

During the winter months, the house was heated by a central steam heating system, and, although electricity was not common in Tennessee until the 1930s, electric lighting illuminated Falcon Rest. There even were telephones!

In 1908, Faulkner also constructed a two-story resort hotel at Faulkner Springs, a fresh water spring located on his property. The spring contained mineral water that was reputed to contain healing properties.

Faulkner died at Falcon Rest in 1916. Mary sold it three years later and moved back to the bustle of city life in Nashville. In 1929, Dr. Herman Reynolds, a physician and dentist, bought the house, and used it as his home and office until his death in 1941.

The house was then turned into a hospital and sanitarium for the elderly called Faulkner Springs Hospital. Operated by Dr. J.P. Dietrich, it was a well-equipped facility for its time, and hundreds of babies were born there, cuts were stitched, and citizens cared for. It became a well-loved part of the town, and everyone seems to have a fond memory of it.

However, by 1968, a more modern hospital was built in McMinnville, and Dr. Deitrich closed down Faulkner Springs Hospital. He gave away all the beds, pulled out the wooden portions of the construction, then attacked the brickwork, trying like the devil to pull the place to the ground. All those brick walls, however, were sunk deeply into the Tennessee bedrock and would not be moved.

The house remained vacant until 1983, when a couple bought it and restored three rooms before selling it to its present owners, George and Charlien McGlothin. The couple have renamed Faulkner's home Falcon Manor and have restored it to its former glorious elegance. Called Tennessee's Biltmore by the Public Television Network, it's now operated as a bed and breakfast, restaurant, and dinner theater.

Daily themed tours are offered to the public. Dinner is included, and customers are invited to join in an interactive show, such as *Murder in the Mansion*, where customers help solve the mystery of who done it.

A tour that has recently been added is the Ghost in the Mansion tour. Although the dinner play includes a whole host of fictional ghostly characters, the tour is more than just a marketing ploy. Reports are the manor has been haunted for decades. The play incorporates the house's ghost stories.

The first mention of otherworldly spirits in Falcon Manor was in 1919, three years after the death of Clay Faulkner. Faulkner's young grandson was playing out in the backyard. He came around to the front, carrying a branch from a tree. He told his parents that a man had given it to him. When asked what the man looked like, he described Faulkner perfectly.

In more recent times, when Charlien's mother, Margaret Piper, was living in the home, heavy footsteps were heard walking in the upstairs hallway. The footsteps would climb the stairs and walk down the hallway to Mrs. Piper's bedroom door, where they stopped. He never seemed to come inside the room, which had been his when he was alive.

George McGlothin's theory on why Faulkner never tried to enter the room when his mother-in-law was there was because Faulkner was a proper Victorian gentleman, and proper Victorian gentlemen would never enter a proper Victorian lady's bedroom uninvited.

After Mrs. Piper died, guests reported strange occurrences, such as objects being moved when the guests were out of the room. The McGlothins stopped letting people stay in the room when a female visitor reported that her lingerie had been tampered with. Maybe old Clay wasn't so proper after all.

According to the McGlothins, he's still around. One recent Christmas, the family was putting up decorations, when they heard someone whistling a

Christmas carol—in perfect pitch. The sound was coming from the stairway. There was, however, no one there.

Another time, McGlothin and some workmen were painting a room, when suddenly a drop cloth that was lying flat on the floor was picked up and lifted high in the air. It stayed there for some time, while McGlothin walked around it. He found no reason for it to be suspended there.

There is another spirit roaming the hallways of Falcon Manor. A woman wearing a high-necked dress and carrying a lantern has been sighted through an upstairs window. She's thought to be the spirit of a Mrs. Morford, who lived there when the place was a sanitarium. She was recovering from bone surgery and spent a lot of time sitting in the parlor.

Maybe it is Mrs. Morford. But why would she be carrying a lantern? Falcon Manor was way ahead of its time, with electricity installed at construction. Besides, the place was a sanitarium in the 1940s, when electricity was commonplace. Still, I guess Mrs. Morford is as good a guess as any!

Finally, a Public Broadcasting Network crew that was filming a show on Falcon Manor had an unusual experience. It was a calm, windless day, and the crew recorded an interview with George out on the porch. When they played the tape back at the studio, they found the sound of wind in the background. The production manager said it sounded as if a hurricane were blowing through, but there had been no wind at all and the equipment was working fine.

Rotherwood Mansion

Tragedy and a history of cruelty have marked this historic private home on the Holston River in eastern Tennessee. Fredrick Ross, founder of the community of Rossville, which later became known as Kingsport, built the mansion in 1818. A successful plantation owner, Ross was a doting father to his daughter, Rowena, a gentle girl whom everyone loved.

Nothing was too good for Rowena as far as her father was concerned. He sent her to the finest Eastern schools and gave her most anything her heart desired. He could not, however, protect her from the tragedy and loss that plagued her throughout her life.

Rowena had been home from school for only a couple of years when she met and fell hopelessly in love with a young man from a nearby town. After their engagement announcement, a grand wedding was planned, and Rowena was the happiest she'd ever been.

The first tragedy of her life struck the day before her wedding. Her young fiancé decided to go fishing on the Holston River with a few friends. Somehow during the trip, the boat capsized and her fiancé drowned.

Despondent, Rowena became a recluse for years, until she finally met someone and fell in love again. This time she did get married, but within a year, her husband died of yellow fever.

It was ten years later before Rowena finally married again. She had a daughter, a little girl that she doted on, just as her father had doted on her. Then tragedy struck once again. Her daughter became ill and died.

Losing her daughter was the last tragedy Rowena could bear. She reportedly drowned herself in the Holston River.

Shortly after her death, a ghostly spirit in a flowing white dress began to be seen. This lady in white, which is assumed to be the spirit of Rowena Ross, has been sighted for more than 125 years, usually wandering the banks of the river where she died.

Prominent Tennesseans John Dennis, a Kingsport financier, and George Eastman have reportedly seen her.

In one report, a young man, who is now a prominent dentist, was picking strawberries in front of Rotherwood Mansion. A feeling that someone was watching him caused him to turn. He found a lady in white standing there. She was ethereal, completely see-through, and he knew at once that he was seeing a ghost. She watched him for several minutes, then disappeared.

Rowena, a gentle spirit, is the mansion's most frequently seen spirit, but there is another spirit that haunts the mansion, one with a much more sinister presence. After Rowena's death, Fredrick Ross experienced financial losses so great that it became necessary for him to sell the mansion.

In 1847, the plantation was sold to Joshua Phipps, a man whom most of the community disliked. Phipps ran the plantation with an iron hand. His cruel treatment of his slaves was notorious, with neighbors reporting hearing the cries of those he was beating. Despite his meanness, the plantation prospered for many years.

Then one summer, the cruel master fell ill with a horrible mysterious illness. Many believed the illness was a result of a curse that Phipps's abused slaves placed on him.

According to legend, a young slave boy was fanning Phipps as he was lying in his bed, when suddenly, huge black flies began landing on his face. The slave boy at first tried to wave the flies away, but finally he stopped fanning and watched in fascination. The flies covered Phipps's face and had crawled into his nose, finally smothering him to death.

After Phipps's death, his spirit began haunting Rotherwood Mansion. Maniacal laughter has been heard echoing through the halls. Ghostly eyes have been seen peering into windows. Other more frightening phenomena have occurred. Sometimes in the night, the covers will be suddenly jerked from the bed, and sleepers awake to Phipps's apparition at the foot of the bed laughing hysterically. A feeling of maliciousness always accompanies these events.

Cragfont Mansion

James Winchester was quite the hero. A distinguished soldier in the Revolutionary War, a brave pioneer and warrior of the hostile frontier, a brigadier general in the War of 1812, and a founder of Memphis, Winchester was a leader in the building of Tennessee.

Construction on Cragfont Mansion, so named because it is built on a rocky bluff with a spring at its base, was begun in 1798, two years after the final Native American battle in the area. It was finished in 1802. The Georgian architecture home was the grandest mansion in the Tennessee frontier. James and his wife, Susan, both lived in the house until their deaths. They are buried in the family cemetery, located on the premises.

When the Civil War broke out, James's youngest son, George Washington Winchester, and wife, Malvina, were living in the mansion. When George went off to war, Malvina took over care of the plantation and kept it running until George's return. Unfortunately, when George returned, the economy of the South was so bad he was forced to sell.

The plantation changed owners numerous times

through the next years until 1958, when the state of Tennessee bought it and made it an historic landmark. It's now open to the public for tours.

Many believe that James Winchester haunts Cragfont Mansion. Candles have been seen burning in the windows at night, and there are reports of ghostly figures peering out the windows. Some say the spirit of Malvina Winchester also still walks the halls of Cragfont, taking care of business just as she did in life.

Millennium Manor

William Nicholson was a devout man with a unique translation of the Bible. He believed that if your faith was strong enough, you'd live forever. Because he was a faithful man, Nicholson knew he'd need a house to last the millennia. So that's what he built.

Drafting his wife, Fair, as his only helper, Nicholson began construction in 1938, at age sixty. After Nicholson's eight-hour shift at the Alcoa plant just across the road from his chosen home site, the couple toiled six to eight hours into the night, hauling great slabs of Tennessee pink marble from a nearby quarry, some weighing as much as three hundred pounds. Nicholson built a ramp and cart to haul the slabs up to the roof.

The sight of the elderly couple hauling tons of rocks up those ramps for hours every night flabbergasted locals. When Fair died of cancer in 1950, many said the grueling hard work had hastened her death. Nicholson just said her faith wasn't strong enough.

Nicholson's two-story, fourteen-room manor is an architectural marvel, with the stone roof and walls set in the same Roman architecture of arches and keystones that survives in buildings two thousand years old. According to experts, this construction method alone might last an eternity. But that didn't satisfy Nicholson. His home had to withstand whatever man could throw at it before Armageddon arrived. That included a nuclear attack.

So he poured more than four thousand bags of concrete and allowed the cement to seep into and around the huge slabs of stone to further reinforce the three-thousand foot structure. The roof is estimated to weigh 432 tons, and is able to withstand the weight of several tanks. The walls are all at least nineteen inches thick, and the floors are four feet thick, with pipe embedded deep within the walls. The house contains all the amenities necessary for a very, very long and happy life, including a sauna and a dungeon. What more could you ask for?

Millennium Manor may well exist forever. Nicholson didn't. At least not in the earthly sense. He died in 1965. There are reports, though, that he is still living there. People claim to have seen his spirit still moving around the property, just as he did in life, and strange lights have been seen floating around the inside of the manor.

Capitol in a State

Capitol in a State

In the beginning, the capital of Tennessee was in Knoxville. But as Tennessee grew, it became obvious that having the capital on the eastern side of the state would cause a hardship for those who lived in West Tennessee. So, in 1819, the capital was moved to the central location of Murfreesboro. It then moved to Nashville in 1826.

For the first twenty years, the legislature met in a small house in Nashville. As the state grew, it finally became obvious that a larger, permanent structure was necessary. Land was purchased on a prominence 175 feet above the river, and William Strickland, the country's preeminent architect, was hired in 1845 to design and build a state capitol building.

Strickland came up with a glorious design. It was to be a three-storied building, made of a special fossiliferous limestone. At either end, there was to be an Ionic portico of eight white columns, each four feet in diameter and thirty-three feet high. At the sides there were to be porticoes of six columns each. A tower was to rise above the center of the roof, 206 feet from the ground. The tower's quadrangle base was to be forty-two feet high, topped by a circular cell thirty-seven feet high with eight fluted Corinthian columns, the design of which was taken from the choragic monument of Lysicrates at Athens.

Whew! Sounded pretty expensive for Tennessee's fledgling budget, but Strickland promised the building would be considered the most handsome in the Union. Fine, the legislators said, but, they stipulated, Strickland had to work closely with Samuel Morgan to keep costs within the budget.

When Strickland agreed, he had no idea just what he was getting into. What could be the problem? He'd build the building in a couple to three years and be gone.

It didn't quite work out that way. From their first meeting, Strickland and Morgan detested each other. They were total opposites. Strickland, an architect of national repute, rarely had to consider budget constraints. Morgan was a notorious penny pincher. The two bickered over everything, from building materials to the expense of the design. They had loud, contentious arguments almost daily. Standing in the midst of unfinished construction, they would scream at each other until they were red-faced and almost apoplectic. Fund shortages and their arguments caused endless construction delays.

The delays drew out completion of the project years over the two-to-three-tops that Strickland originally had in mind. He, in fact, did not live to see the 1859 completion of the Tennessee Capitol building. In 1854, Strickland, who was in failing health, suffered a fatal fall.

In concurrence with Strickland's wishes, the state agreed to have him interred within the Capitol building. A vault was built above the building's cornerstone, and his body was placed there.

After Strickland's death, Morgan took over construction and, with the assistance of Strickland's son, completed the building. Just as Strickland predicted, the Tennessee Capitol building was hailed as an extraordinary triumph. It was considered one of the most magnificent buildings of its time.

That's not the end of the story, of course. Morgan died in 1880, and to honor him and his work on the Capitol building, the state fathers saw fit to have him interred on the building's southeast corner. Oops!

Two recent incidents show that in death, Strickland and Morgan have resumed their animosity toward each other. In each incident, a rookie Nashville police officer was called to the Capitol building on a disturbance. And in each incident, the officer reported hearing the sounds of two men in a heated argument, yelling and cursing at each other. Investigations of the area revealed no one around.

When the rookies reported the events, veteran Nashville officers said, "Oh, no big deal." They explained that in the years since Morgan was interred inside the building, other police officers had experienced the same exact thing. Many had heard the sounds of a loud argument between two men, only to find upon investigation that the place was deserted.

Ironic, isn't it, that in attempting to honor these two men, who in life detested each other, state officials doomed them to an eternity together?

The Haunting of Loretta Lynn

The Haunting of Loretta Lynn

In the country music industry, Loretta Lynn is legendary. Even if you're not a country music fan, you probably know her from *Coal Miner's Daughter*, the Oscar-winning movie about her life.

She was born dirt poor in Butcher Hollow, Kentucky, the daughter of a coal miner. She was married at age thirteen to a man who, recognizing her singing and songwriting talents, took her to Nashville in search of fame and fortune. There were many hardships on the way, but talent won out, and she sailed by rich and famous, right on into country music legend.

Her heyday was in the 1960s and 1970s, when she wrote and sang songs about the struggles and happiness of everyday life. She sang about heartache, but it was heartache with triumph—strong women living their lives and dealing with adversity. Her songs dealt with marriage, children, and divorce. Drinking and cheating husbands were put on notice. Her song "One's On The Way" spoke to the woman overwhelmed by kids, housework, and negligent husbands.

As much notice as those songs brought her, they couldn't compare to her song "The Pill," which talked about a woman discovering the advantages of easy birth control. The song caused much controversy and was banned from many radio stations, but that didn't keep women from listening to it and heeding its message.

Because she related to everyday situations that common people faced, Loretta became one of the most well known women of her time. Her name was frequently found on polls seeking to identify the most admired women in the country; she kept company with world leaders and others in positions of power and prestige. But she never changed from the unpretentious manner with which she approached life, even daring to address Richard Nixon by his first name when she appeared at the White House in the early 1970s.

One reason Lynn was able to tune into the lives of everyday people might be the fact that she possesses psychic abilities, a talent she believes she inherited from her mother. Throughout the years, she's experienced premonitions that have come to pass.

These experiences began when she was a fourteen-year-old bride, pregnant, and far away from home. The bond she had with her mother was a strong one, and often one could sense when the other was feeling lonely and depressed, and that a letter was in order. So in tune was she with her mother and her feelings that Lynn could accurately predict on what day she would receive a letter from her and vice versa.

One of the strongest premonitions Lynn had concerned her father. One day, when she was away on tour, Lynn had a sudden vision of him in his coffin and of her attending his funeral. The next day, she learned her father had died of a massive stroke. The story is told that years later, she returned to the home where she grew up and saw the ghost of her father sitting comfortably on the front porch.

In another devastating loss, Loretta was on tour when her son, Jack Benny, lost his life in a river when he was thirty years old. She apparently suffered a seizure, and subsequently could not remember anything for days. At the same time the young man's body was found, she came out of the condition, instinctively saying to her husband, "It's Jack Benny, isn't it."

A much happier intuition occurred in 1967, when Lynn and husband "Doo" were in the market for a bigger home for their growing family. They were out driving around Tennessee one day, when they took a wrong turn and ended up on a back road near the small town of Hurricane Mills. That's where they found the home that Lynn knew straight away was just the right place. And they found that not only was the place a beautiful plantation home, but the charming little town of Hurricane Mills also was included in the sale price.

Sold!

Ghosts on the Plantation

It wasn't long after the Lynns moved into their new home that they learned they weren't the only ones living there. OK, maybe "living" is not exactly the right word. First, Loretta began to notice that the adjoining door between her twin daughters' rooms would open and close by itself. Next, the girls reported seeing a woman in their bedrooms—a woman dressed in old-fashioned clothing with her hair piled up on her head.

Daughter Peggy later told interviewers about being three or four years old and lying in bed one night, when she felt someone watching her. She turned to see a lady in white coming from the bathroom. She said she remembers wondering if someone was visiting, but then the lady took a couple of steps backward and just disappeared.

Loretta saw the lady herself one day. It happened when she was just returning from a tour. She looked up to see a woman in an old-fashioned white dress standing on the second-floor balcony. The woman was crying and wringing her hands. Like Peggy, Loretta mistook the lady in white for a guest, and when she entered the house, she quizzed the girl's nanny on who was visiting. No one was the reply. Loretta stepped back outside in time to see the woman in white walking through the cemetery that's on the property.

Curious, Loretta did a little research on the history of her home. She found that Beulah Anderson, one of the original owners, had given birth to a stillborn child, and a few days later, Beulah had died as well. The two are buried side by side in the cemetery. Loretta believes the lady in white is Beulah, still grieving and searching for her child.

Loretta's research also revealed that a small Civil War skirmish had been fought on the plantation in

July 1863. Nineteen Confederate soldiers had been killed and are buried in the cemetery. In light of other occurrences experienced by the Lynn family, that information made sense.

Most of the incidents occurred in the room the family called the Brown Room. It was a place in which no one felt comfortable. It was always several degrees colder than any other room in the house, and for some reason no one understood, big, black flies were always found dead on the windowsill. This phenomenon occurs nowhere else in the house. Several frightening events have occurred in the Brown Room.

The first incident occurred not long after the family moved in. Son Jack Benny said he was sound asleep in the room when he suddenly awoke to find a Confederate soldier standing at the foot of the bed. The soldier was tugging on Jack's boot, which he'd fallen asleep wearing. Terrified, the boy ran out of the room and refused to sleep there ever again.

A similar incident happened to Ernest, another of Loretta's sons. He, too, was sleeping when he was awakened by the feeling that he was being watched. Someone was. When he opened his eyes, he saw two Confederate soldiers standing there, staring at him. He pulled a Jack and ran from the room, vowing never to sleep there again.

Others have sighted Confederate soldiers on the grounds. A fisherman once reported looking up from his endeavors on the river to see a soldier walking across the bridge. As the fisherman watched, the soldier just disappeared. Another time, a guest reported seeing two soldiers sitting beside a ghostly fire.

Once a working plantation, Lynn's Hurricane Mills plantation unfortunately used slaves for labor. One of the most bizarre features of the house was the "slave pit," a dark and dank cellar with an iron grate over the top. Located underneath the front porch, the pit was reportedly used as punishment for disobedient slaves, who endured much pain, chained inside its dank interior.

One night, Lynn and a friend were watching television when they heard someone walking across the front porch. Thinking someone was coming to visit, they turned on the porch light and looked expectantly outside. No one was there. Puzzled, they sat back down and started watching television again. The sound came again—only this time, it sounded as if someone were dragging chains across the porch. Upon investigating, they realized that the sounds were coming from the old slave pit.

In response to all the supernatural happenings, Lynn decided to conduct a séance in order to make contact with the spirits living with her. During the séance, a ghost identifying himself as "Anderson" made contact. But when the group tried to elicit more information, he seemed to get upset. As they asked him a series of questions, the large wooden table they were sitting around began to shake violently. Rising off the floor and into the air, it suddenly dropped heavily back to the floor and broke in two. James Anderson, of course, was the name of the original owner. He, too, is buried in the plantation cemetery. Lynn's not sure why he was so angry during the séance, but she says she's not going to try to contact him again!

He's made himself known in other incidents, however. In one such episode, a tour guide inadvertently brushed against a framed album cover hanging on the wall of the staircase and knocked it askew. She had stopped the tour to give a short presentation and was standing on the next to the last step. She was interrupted by one of the group, who asked who the man was standing behind her. At that moment, she was pushed off the steps.

Lynn believes that man was Anderson and that he was taking care of the place, upset that the guide had moved the album. When she first realized the house was haunted, she said, she had a little talk with the ghosts and told them she'd fix the place up real nice and take care of it. She feels that there is a mutual respect and that Anderson doesn't like the albums touched. He just mostly likes to show up to aggravate folks. Lynn believes Anderson helps look after her because he knows she won't let anything happen to the house.

Now in her seventies, Lynn still writes songs, performs, and records. She loves her Hurricane Mills plantation, the home she felt so drawn to all those years ago. And she doesn't mind sharing it with those who've loved it before her.

Maybe, years in the future, there'll come a time when the next owner tells the tale of a spirit he's seen walking the halls of the Hurricane Mills plantation. It was, he'll say, the spirit of a beautiful woman with long brown hair, sparkling eyes, and a magnificent smile. She was wearing a glittering dress and strumming a guitar.

"She didn't mean any harm," he'll say. "She was just watching over the place."

Andrew and Rachel Jackson: A Love Story of the Ages

Andrew and Rachel Jackson: A Love Story of the Ages

The story of Andrew Jackson's rise to the presidency of the United States is an interesting story, no doubt—full of valor, full of patriotism. But the story of Jackson's love life is an even more interesting tale. It has everything—sex, lies, scandal, and, best of all, undying love.

Andrew Jackson was born on March 15, 1767, in the Waxhaws, on the border of North and South Carolina. His father was killed in a logging accident just a month before Andrew was born. His mother, by all accounts a strong and independent woman, raised Andrew and his two older brothers in South Carolina at the home of her sister.

Even before the signing of the Declaration of Independence, Jackson, who was nine years old, had an abiding hate for the British because of stories his mother told of her days in Ireland, and the suffering experienced at the hands of the British. His experiences during the American Revolution only served to deepen his hate.

Jackson joined the Continental Army as a courier at age thirteen. One of his older brothers was killed in 1779. Andrew and brother, Robert, were taken prisoner for several weeks in 1781. While incarcerated, the boys were ordered to clean the boots of a British officer. When they refused, the officer struck them with his sword, cutting Andrew's hand to the bone.

Both Andrew and Robert contracted smallpox, and Robert died within days of their release. That same year, Jackson's mother died, and, at age fourteen, he found he had lost his entire family. He spent the next year and a half living with relatives.

At about the same age, Rachel Donelson was traveling with her parents on a flatboat called the *Adventure*. Her father was leading a crew of family and friends westward. The convoy traveled more than a thousand miles to Fort Nashborough, now known as Nashville, the last outpost on the American Frontier.

The family didn't stay long in Fort Nashborough, where Native American attacks were becoming more frequent and more violent. They moved on to Harrodsburg, Kentucky, a more civilized area, where seventeen-year-old Rachel married Lewis Robards. Their marriage was turbulent, and by 1788, Rachel returned alone to her mother's home, which was now back in Fort Nasborough.

In that same year, young Andrew Jackson, now a certified attorney, traveled from Salisbury, North Carolina, to Fort Nasborough, where he stayed in a boarding home owned by Rachel's mother, now a widow. It's here that Andrew and Rachel met, beginning their love of the ages.

Since Rachel was still married to Robards (the couple had tried to reconcile several times), Andrew and Rachel's relationship began as a friendship. Rachel's relationship with Robards fell apart after he falsely accused Rachel and Andrew of an affair. Andrew, notorious for his chivalry, confronted the angry husband about his treatment of Rachel, which Andrew believed to be abuse. After the confrontation, Andrew moved out of the boarding home and Robards left for Kentucky—without Rachel.

Weeks later, word reached Rachel that Robards was coming to claim her and return her to Kentucky with him. Having had enough of her husband's unreasonable jealousy and abuse, Rachel decided to flee to Natchez, Mississippi, to avoid returning to Kentucky with her husband.

Hearing of Rachel's plans, Andrew expressed dismay for "innocently and unintentionally causing the loss of peace and happiness of Mrs. Robards, whom he believed to be a fine woman."

Andrew's next action, however, may have belied his innocence, at least in heart, toward his relationship with Rachel. Despite being named as the third party in a marital affair, Andrew announced his plans to accompany Rachel on her river voyage to Natchez. This action confirmed Robards's suspicions about an affair, and gave him the evidence he needed to begin divorce proceedings.

Andrew brought Rachel the news that her husband was divorcing her. Thinking she was divorced, Andrew asked for her hand in marriage and she accepted. In 1791, the couple returned to Tennessee as husband and wife. Ahh, but all was not well.

After almost two years of wedded bliss, the young couple (both twenty-six) learned that—oops!—Rachel was still married to Robards. Seems the cad had only obtained permission from the General Assembly of Virginia to apply for divorce, but had neglected to bring the divorce to court.

There has been much speculation on why Robards

waited so long to bring the divorce to court. Some thought maybe he had hoped for a reconciliation, though two years and a marriage would seem to be a clue that it wasn't going to happen. Some thought perhaps he hoped to share in Rachel's late father's estate; some thought it was revenge against the couple for wounding his pride.

Still others thought it was simply a matter of ignorance. Divorce was a new concept at that time and maybe Robards just didn't know the procedures. Regardless of why, Robards was finally awarded a divorce in 1793, after the Kentucky courts found Rachel guilty of adultery and desertion.

Andrew and Rachel were married again in Nashville. They had a strong union and were deeply in love, but the divorce and remarriage caused a scandal that haunted them for the rest of their lives.

The couple settled in Nashville, first in Hunter's Hill Plantation, where Andrew ran the Hunter's Hill General Store. In July 1804, Andrew bought the farm adjoining his Hunter's Hill Plantation for $3,400, selling his more valuable plantation to satisfy outstanding debts.

Andrew immediately hired workmen to spruce up

the new farmhouse with French wallpaper and paint. He had the fields cleared and fences built, and by August, he and Rachel had moved into their Rural Retreat, a name he almost immediately changed to the Hermitage. The farm was initially operated as a small cotton farm, with nine slaves. By 1820, Andrew had grown the farm into a profitable thousand-acre plantation, with a distillery, a dairy, cotton gin and press, and slave cabins for the plantation's forty-four slaves.

In addition to the cash cotton crop and the produce grown to feed the family, which now included an adopted child they named Andrew Jr., and its slaves, the Hermitage also served as an indulgence for Andrew's passion for race horses. He and Rachel lived in the small farm house until the winter of 1820, when they moved into the two-story brick Federal-style home Andrew had built for his family. Rachel decorated her new home with wallpapers imported from France depicting Greek mythology themes.

The couple loved their home and considered it a work in progress. They were constantly improving the house and grounds, investing in brick homes for the mansion's slaves and adding formal gardens for Rachel.

If it hadn't been for Andrew's political aspirations,

Rachel and Andrew may have lived a long and happy life, growing old together and rocking away their twilight years on the veranda of the Hermitage. But he did have aspirations, setting his sights on the highest office in the land.

Andrew lost his first bid for the presidency in what he and his supporters called the Stolen Election. He had won the popular vote hands down, but did not have enough electoral votes to win outright. His opponents, who thought him an uneducated bumpkin, conspired to throw the election to John Quincy Adams.

The circumstances of Andrew's and Rachel's courtship and marriage returned to haunt them when Andrew again ran for president in 1828. The Adams camp resurrected the adultery and desertion charges against Rachel. The malicious gossip caused her much embarrassment and pain. The stress, Andrew was convinced, contributed to her early death.

Rachel Jackson died suddenly on December 22, 1828, just one month after Andrew won the presidential election. Andrew decided to bury her in her favorite place on Earth—her gardens at the Hermitage. He had a small frame building erected over her burial crypt until a more fitting monument could be constructed.

In 1831, Andrew hired an architect to remodel the Hermitage and build a tomb for Rachel and for him. The tomb strongly resembled a Greek temple found on the wallpaper Rachel had picked out for the Hermitage entrance hall. The tomb was finished in 1832, and Andrew, still in Washington, wrote home daily to his adopted son, directing him to restore the gardens, which had declined after Rachel's death.

Returning to the Hermitage in 1837, in failing health, Andrew visited Rachel daily at the tomb whenever possible. When his health would not allow a visit, he could easily see the tomb from both his bedroom and office windows. On June 8, 1845, Andrew joined Rachel in death. He was laid to rest beside her two days later.

The story of Andrew and Rachel Jackson is a love story that spans the ages. According to legend, it's a story that lives on. The couple has reportedly been sighted wandering around the plantation grounds. They have been seen most often strolling hand in hand through Rachel's formal gardens.

The sightings of Andrew and Rachel began after

restoration of the Hermitage. After Andrew's death, the Hermitage had gone to Andrew Jr., but he was unable to keep the property. He sold it to the state of Tennessee in 1856. Because of budget constraints and the Civil War, the property was allowed to deteriorate until 1889. During that year, the state commissioned the Ladies Hermitage Association to take over the property and its restoration.

When the ladies first began renovations, no caretaker was available and, worried that vandals would strike, several of the group agreed to stay at the house. The first night, after a quick dinner and a nice evening rocking on the porch, the ladies settled in for the night on a mattress in the parlor.

They were sleeping peacefully until the dead middle of the night when a loud clattering sound suddenly awakened them. It was coming from the kitchen, and it was as if someone was throwing all the pots and pans onto the floor and slamming cabinet doors.

The din grew to include the clanging of chains on the porch and a pounding, as if Andrew Jackson himself were riding his trusty steed up and down the stairs. Terrified, the ladies lit a kerosene lamp and the sounds stopped just as suddenly as they had started. They didn't sleep a wink the rest of the night, but the noises did not return.

The next morning they walked through the entire house, but could find no reason for the strange sounds they had heard. The day was passed peacefully, and that night, the ladies left a light burning beside the bed. That didn't help, though. Around midnight, the sounds started again, beginning with the clanging in the kitchen, escalating to the dragging of chains across the porch, and culminating with the sound of the horse charging up and down the stairs.

These sounds returned every night for the week the ladies stayed. At the end of the week, thankfully, a caretaker was found to stay on the property, though not inside the house. The ladies didn't talk about their experiences at the Hermitage until years later. No explanation was ever found.

About the Author

Lynne L. Hall is a native Southerner who is well acquainted with the people and places that make these stories so interesting to read and share. Her work has appeared in *Cosmopolitan*, *Penthouse*, *Popular Science*, *Physical*, and in many other magazines. She is the author of the Strange But True series of books that includes volumes on Alabama, Florida, Georgia, Virginia, and Tennessee.

Other ghostly tales from Lynne's pen are found in *Florida Ghosts*, *North Carolina Ghosts*, and *South Carolina Ghosts*.